UNDERSTANDING SOCIAL ISSUES

DIVORCE

Liz Friedrich

D1349243

GLOUCESTER PRESS
London : New York : Toronto : Sydney

In most societies where there is marriage there is divorce. Divorce marks the legal end to a marriage which has broken down and deals with arrangements for the care of children and the rearrangement of a couple's finances. It leaves the partners free to marry again.

At present there are rising divorce rates everywhere in the developed world. During the 1980s one in every three marriages ends in divorce in Britain where in 1986 there were 394,000 marriages and 180,000 divorces. In some parts of the United States, one in two marriages ends in divorce. "Marriage is in decline" say some people – the divorce rate is a symptom of society's moral degeneracy. But is it? Or is it that we are living in a time of social change when marriage and family patterns are altering? Others argue that liberal divorce laws lead to more marriage breakdown. True? Or does it mean that the divorce rate more closely reflects the number of marriages which break down?

Our society has a confused attitude towards divorce: accepting it as inevitable but at the same time hankering after the religious ideal of "'til death us do part"; it deplores marriage breakdown but at the same time puts few resources into supporting couples with problems, or caring for families where a marriage has broken up.

To understand some of these issues, this book looks at how our divorce laws have evolved; how marriage has changed and the effects of divorce on both adults and children.

Marriage is an important ceremony in every society. This young Hungarian couple hope to spend a lifetime together but 40 per cent of marriages in Hungary end in divorce.

CHAPTER 1

MARRIAGE – CHANGING ATTITUDES

"One night I got out the wedding photos and cried. There was this bright young couple. We looked so in love, we'd hoped for so much. How did it go so wrong?"

When a marriage ends it is because it has in some way failed to meet the expectations of one or both partners. What is expected from marriage is largely governed by the culture in which we live.

Arranged marriage
In an arranged marriage, common in Asian, Greek, Turkish and Jewish communities, it is expected that love will follow marriage, not precede it. A young couple may have the final say in a choice of a partner but they trust their parents to make wise choices in selecting possible partners from a suitable background. In an arranged marriage it is not just two individuals but two families who are becoming related. The couple have a great deal of support, often financial as well as emotional. If there are problems the family will rally round to help resolve them. At its best the system offers great support. At its worst it can put pressure on individuals to stay in an unhappy situation. The system of arranged marriage is under pressure in some societies from young people influenced by Western ideas.

> **"My friends don't understand how I can allow my parents to arrange a marriage for me. But my sisters had arranged marriages and I can see they work."**

All you need is love
Although the idea of the arranged marriage seems quite alien to 20th century Western societies it is not so long ago that arranged marriages were the norm among the land-owning classes in Europe.

Even at the beginning of this century couples were likely to be drawn from a fairly restricted social and geographical area. The two families probably already knew one another. A young man expected to ask his "intended's" father for his daughter's hand in marriage and to be able to answer questions about his ability to support a wife and family. When a couple married they usually remained in their own community near their families.

By the 1960s, it seemed that all you needed was love. Today people decide for themselves who to marry and when. They may choose to live far away from parents and value establishing a separate, independent existence. Marriage is expected to fulfil every sexual and emotional need. It is portrayed as an adventure together, where each partner can find individual growth and satisfaction. The reality for many couples may be rather different. Nevertheless many couples still believe the romantic ideal.

This Hindu couple may have met only a few times before the wedding ceremony. They expect love to come after, not before, marriage.

Till death us do part

In 1986, Elle (a British fashion magazine) carried out a survey and found that 71 per cent of married couples, and the majority of those who were divorced, thought that marriage should be a lifetime commitment. No one who gets married plans to get divorced, but a lifetime together has become a long time, up to 50 years. In the 17th century most marriages ended after about 17 years with the death of one partner. But should we expect today's relationships to last a lifetime? Has divorce replaced death as a way of changing partners?

> "Love in books and films is fine but they don't show what happens after marriage. People don't just live happily ever after."

Women's independence

Perhaps the biggest social change this century has been in the lives of women. But what effect has this had on the nature of marriage? For centuries women's lives were dominated by child-bearing and child-rearing. In 1900 a young woman could expect to live until she was 66 and she would spend 20 years of her life devoted to having and caring for babies. By 1950 her life expectancy had risen to 75 and she was spending only about six years caring for small children. Widely available, efficient contraception has reduced the average number of children in a family from six at the beginning of the century to under two in the 1980s.

Released from child-bearing, women have been finding paid employment. In the 1930s fewer than

10 per cent of married women were in paid employment. Today, over 50 per cent of married women are in employment.

> "One night I got out the wedding photos and cried. There was this bright young couple. We looked so in love, we'd hoped for so much. How did it go so wrong?"

Women's wages are far from reaching equality with those of men and many, because of family responsibilities, work part-time. Nevertheless they have a financial independence undreamt of little more than 100 years ago when the law, along with the church, regarded husband and wife as "one flesh" - his. A wife had no property or income of her own, it all belonged to her husband. Women won the right to divorce on the same terms as men in the 1920s. But it was only as they spent less time in child-bearing and gained some financial independence that they began to have a real choice.

More and more married women are working outside the home. They no longer need to be completely financially dependent on a husband.

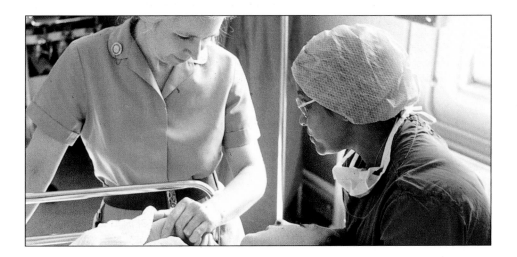

"My grand-daughter has a family and works full-time. I worked full-time too but it was washing and cooking, sewing and mending – no labour-saving machines in my day."

Changing roles?

Articles in glossy magazines – depicting the smart business woman striding off to a challenging job in the city while her house-husband stays at home to care for 1.8 children – are far from the lives of most ordinary people. It is sometimes said that there are two marriages - his and hers. His has not changed very much. A few generations back he worked full-time in paid employment and she worked full-time at home caring for him and their children. Now he works full-time in paid employment and she works full or part-time in paid employment and still cares for the children and for him. She may also be responsible for an elderly relative. It has been estimated that on average in Europe, a woman has only two-thirds of the free time that her husband has.

In a few countries such as Sweden, both parents have a legal right to time off to care for children. Yet in most countries it is still assumed that children are primarily the mother's responsibility. Some couples arrange their working lives so that they take an equal share of child-care.

Fathers who are involved in caring for their children are becoming more common. But in most families it is still the women who are responsible for the cooking, washing and cleaning as well as childcare.

"When we had our second child he assumed it would be me that gave up work to stay at home. I resented that. That was when things started to go wrong."

CHAPTER 2

WHO GETS DIVORCED?

Nearly all these
people will be
married at some
time in their lives.
Around one third
of their marriages
will end in
divorce. Of those
who re-marry,
over half will go
through a second
divorce.

Those who marry while still in their teens are more likely to become divorced. A girl who marries under the age of twenty is twice as likely to become divorced as her friend who marries between the ages of 20 and 24 and three times as likely as a woman marrying between 25 and 29. The kinds of problems young couples are likely to encounter make them vulnerable. A teenage bride may be pregnant; the couple may earn little; they may be unemployed or have unsatisfactory housing. They may be marrying to get away from their parents. With little or no support from parents, they are especially likely to divorce.

Couples who marry late are also more likely to divorce. While young couples may find that as they grow older they grow apart, older couples may find it hard to adapt and grow together. Like young couples, they may find themselves isolated and out of step with their friends. The teenage mother's friends are still single and fancy-free, the older couple are surrounded by nappies when their friends are waving goodbye to their children.

Couples with a low income, who are in unskilled jobs or where one or both of the partners is unemployed, are also more likely to divorce. Couples in this situation may own little property and a wife may not be much worse off on her own drawing state benefit. It is not surprising that many of these marriages end unhappily.

"Both sets of parents thought we were too young to marry but we knew we were right for each other. And we were for about three years."

Second time around

Another group more likely to divorce are those who have already divorced and marry again. An increasing number of divorced people re-marry. In 1970, 18 per cent of marriages involved a partner, or partners, who had been married before. In 1986, re-marriage accounted for one-third of all marriages in Britain. Sadly, for many couples

Love's young dream. But is it a sound basis for a lasting marriage? The younger you marry, the more likely you are to become divorced.

trying again is not necessarily more successful. Twice as many re-marriages as first marriages end in divorce.

The pressures on a second marriage are many – especially for women. For them a second marriage may seem to be the only way out of an existing marriage. If a woman has young children and no job, she has little hope of financial independence and the choices may seem to be to stay put, rely on social security, or re-marry. A hasty re-marriage may not leave one or both partners time to reflect on, or learn from, their previous marriage. They may fall back into old patterns and repeat the same difficulties. They may also not have had time to detach themselves properly from their previous spouse. Problems from the first marriage can intrude into the second.

> **"I felt he'd rescued me from the disaster of my first marriage. I was determined not to repeat the same mistakes. But I hadn't realised how difficult it would be."**

If both partners have children, then they may have problems trying to weld two families into one. If only one partner has children, the new spouse may have problems with becoming an instant (step)parent.

With one marriage a failure, partners often come together with unrealistically high hopes of a second marriage, believing they will get everything right this time. High expectations place an extra pressure on the marriage.

Time to say goodbye

Over a quarter of couples who divorce do so after being married for less then five years. Some of these will have been second marriages which, when they end in divorce, do so more quickly than first marriages. Couples without children get

This is the kind of happy family that most people would like to be part of. It may take hard work to achieve it.

divorced on average eight years after getting married and couples with children, 11 years. There are a number of couples who stay in a difficult marriage until their children are well into their teens. But the trend, since it has become possible to divorce one year after marriage, has been for more couples to divorce more quickly and the proportion of childless couples divorcing is increasing.

Changing explanations

At a time when the divorce rate was low, divorce was seen as a moral issue. The guilty party had behaved badly or had moral defects. The law reflected this attitude which was based on the churches' view of the sacred nature of marriage and adultery as sinful. By the 1950s psychological explanations were popular. Those who divorced had personal problems: they were immature, had failed to adjust to marriage or had chosen the wrong partner.

It was only as the rate of divorce increased dramatically that it was seen as a social issue which reflected changes taking place in society. However, it is still not possible to assess accurately the effects on the divorce rate of social changes such as longer life expectancy and the changing role of women. That has to be left to future sociologists and historians. Nevertheless statistics can measure some of the specific factors that lead to certain groups of people being more likely to divorce.

> **"I might have come to terms with the boyfriend but she started going out every night."**

Grounds for divorce

Increasingly it is women who sue for divorce. In 1986 as in 1985, 72 per cent of divorces were sought by wives. "Unreasonable behaviour" was the most common ground, followed by adultery (a sexual relationship between one of the marriage partners and someone outside of the marraige). The men who sued for divorce gave adultery as the most common reason. Is adultery seen as more significant by men? Do the old attitudes linger on? As a society we have an ambivalent attitude: in an international survey in 1981, 78 per cent of the British questioned still thought adultery was wrong but thought that only 25 per cent of other people abided by the rule.

The grounds chosen for divorce can only give us limited information as to why couples split up. When the divorce law was drawn up, legislators had to find a way of defining the breakdown of a marriage. Adultery, unreasonable behaviour, separation and desertion were the definitions they selected and so anyone seeking a divorce has to make their situation fit what the law requires. People choose the most convenient explanation and that which most approximates the truth. Unreasonable behaviour can cover a great many situations. What defines it is the attitude of the person who has to tolerate it. Attitudes to issues such as money, violence and drinking will vary from one individual to another, and from one social group to another. What is unacceptable to one is shrugged off as normal by another.

Making the break
Although more women than men petition for divorce, it does not mean that they necessarily take the final step to end the marriage. What appears from the few studies that have been made of divorcing couples is that in many of their marriages there are early difficulties which are ignored at the time but emerge later. Couples rarely seek help for difficulties that are longstanding, though

women are more likely than men to seek marriage counselling from organisations such as Marriage Guidance (recently re-named Relate) in Britain.

It usually takes a specific incident or event: a new job, a spell away from home, illness, unemployment or a family crisis to jolt one or both partners into re-assessing their relationship. The most dramatic event is of course one partner falling in love with someone else. Whatever triggers the realisation that the marriage is unsatisfactory, once it is seen in this way everything about the relationship and partner seems wrong. The aggrieved partner wonders why it has taken so long to realise how bad things were. Family and friends ask the same question. In talking, perhaps for the first time, about problems, verbal or even physical abuse is discovered not to be the norm. Despite the so-called permissive society, the nuclear family is a very private one and we have really very little idea about how other people conduct their lives.

> **"After 15 years she was suddenly like a stranger. I couldn't believe it was our marriage she was talking about."**

With two babies and a toddler as well as poor housing, this couple are under a great deal of stress. If they already have some problems in their relationship they could be heading for divorce.

Once a couple or one partner sees the marriage in such a negative way it is very difficult to repair it. Some couples seek help from marriage guidance at this stage. Others talk endlessly with friends or family. When there are children involved a couple will often "try again". Sometimes a couple can work through their problems and achieve a stronger relationship but more often it is too late.

CASE STUDY

Pauline and John's story illustrates how confusing
the process of deciding on divorce can be.

Pauline and John were married in 1965. Pauline remembers the first few years as happy.

"We were both working and quite well off, holidays in Spain, we had a lot of fun".

Mark was born in 1969 and Gary two years later.

"I gave up my job in a bank when Mark was born. I was over the moon. I really like babies and I was happy looking after them. I suppose we didn't go out that much when they were small. John and I got on all right, we didn't fight but then we didn't do much of anything. Our sex life wasn't up to much, it just faded away somehow".

When Mark moved on to secondary school Pauline got a part-time job as a cashier.

"I had to retrain, I was terrified, I had lost all my confidence. But after a bit I really enjoyed being back. John grumbled because I was working longer hours. We had a real fight when I suggested he iron his own shirts.

"It was when I began to get involved with a man at work that I realised just what a state my marriage was in. Being with someone I could talk to, who was interested in me made me feel like I hadn't done for years. One night in front of the TV I looked at John and thought 'that's it, where is my life going. I want a divorce'. I didn't say anything then. For the next few months I was in a real state. I stopped seeing the other man. I tried to talk to John about our relationship, but it was no good. Finally I told him I wanted a divorce. What a scene. We talked then more than we'd done in years, but it was too late. He was so angry, accused me of all kinds of things, even hit me but he said he wanted us to try again.

"I agreed we would give it two months. He was alternately very considerate and very angry, basically he felt I was breaking up a happy home. After five weeks I couldn't stand it any more and I took the kids to my Mum's.

"After that he gave up and I applied for a divorce. It was only then that I found out that he had

had an affair with another woman. I couldn't believe it. He said it was my fault, that I'd had no time for him when I was wrapped up in the babies. I suppose he was right about that in a way. But I felt so angry that he'd been deceiving me for years. In the end we got divorced on the grounds of his adultery, it was the easiest thing".

The couple were divorced in 1981 and the boys lived with their mother.

"John and I were still pretty angry with each other. We did manage to make reasonable arrangements for him to see the boys. I have a boyfriend but I don't think the boys could cope with me re-marrying, not yet anyhow".

CHAPTER 3

HOW THE LAW EVOLVED

"Love in books
and films is fine
but they don't
show what
happens after
marriage. People
don't just live
happily ever
after."

The history of divorce is one of a gradual move towards equality between rich and poor and between men and women. The American legal system is based on British law so British and American divorce laws share the same history.

For hundreds of years, the church regulated marriage. Permanent separation was allowed in cases of adultery but no divorce and re-marriage.

In the days before records of marriage or the existence of a police force a poor man who wanted to end his marriage could simply desert his wife, move to another part of the country and marry again. Bigamy (being married to two women at the same time) was quite common. There were also a number of folk customs such as the "wife sale" where a man symbolically sold his wife for a few pence or pounds. The community then regarded them both as free to re-marry.

"My parents divorced in the 1930s. My father had to provide 'evidence' by taking a woman to the hotel and making sure the chambermaid saw them in bed. It was sordid."

One law for the rich . . .

For the rich, marriage was largely about political alliances between land-owning families. In the 16th and 17th centuries in Europe, the rich employed lawyers to find loopholes in the church law to allow them to have their marriages annulled (declared invalid). The main concern of a land-owner was to have a legitimate heir to inherit his land. If his wife was unfaithful, she could have another man's child. Therefore a wife's adultery

was regarded as far more serious than that of a husband. This was reflected in the first matrimonial laws in the 1850s which made divorce available to men on the grounds of a wife's adultery while women had to prove adultery and exceptionally outrageous behaviour. It was not until the 1920s that women could obtain divorce on the same grounds as men.

The divorce laws in Britain and the United States require one partner to petition for divorce by accusing the other partner of some kind of misconduct. This set up the "adversarial system", where each partner, represented by their lawyers, argues out a settlement. This still underlies the system today. However, in Britain, if divorce is not defended, that is both partners agree to legally end their marriage, divorce can by obtained "by post" without legal assistance or attending the court – providing there are no children involved.

This aristocratic looking French couple stayed together until death. However, he would have been wealthy enough to afford a divorce but his poorer countrymen would not have been able to afford the legal fees.

Landgericht Hamburg

U r t e i l

Im Namen des Volkes!

In der Sache

<table>
<tr><td>Verkündet
am 2. Mai 1963
gez. Schulze,
Justizangestellte,
als Urkundsbeamtin
der Geschäftsstelle.</td><td>der Sekretärin Elke B e r g m a n n
geb. Hinz, Hamburg-Uhlenhorst, Kanal-
strasse 35,</td></tr>
</table>

Klägerin,

Prozessbevollmächtigter:
Rechtsanwalt .... August, Hamburg 1,

g e g e n

ihren Eh......................lten
Walter ...
Uhlenh...

Proze...
Rech...

er...
ka...

Landgericht Hamburg
Urteil
Im Namen des Volkes

Die Ehe der ...teien w... ...age und
Widerklage aus beiderseitigem Verschulden
...schieden.

Die Parteien haben am ....üttel
1 die Ehe miteinande.. 43,
der Kläger am 18. Fe.. .... an-
gehörige und gehöre.. .... Parteien ist ein Kind .. .. 961 ge-
borene Peter. Der .. .. eit
Februar 1963 lebe.. .... rasse
35 dadurch voneinander g... .... nelichen
Wohnung bewohnt.

Die Klägerin möchte geschieden werde... ....agte
habe für sie kein persönliches Interesse meh... ..... eigenen
Wege und behandele sie völlig lieblos. Sie räum... ..... seits auch
den Beklagten nicht die gehörige Aufmerksamkeit entgeg... ...acht zu haben. Der Beklagte seinerseits macht mit der Widerklage gel... ...nd, dass die
Klägerin ihn vernachlässigt und sich nicht um ihn gekümmert habe. Sie

CHAPTER 4

THE LEGAL PROCESS

"However well
you behave to
start with, the law
turns it into a
battle. The way
they call it
'Johnson versus
Johnson', you
know there's
expected to be a
fight."

A number of reforms of British divorce laws this century ended finally in the Divorce Reform Act in 1969 which established the only basis for divorce as the "irretrievable breakdown of marriage". Either spouse can petition for divorce and must show evidence of the breakdown of the marriage under one of five headings.

- their partner has committed adultery and the spouse finds it intolerable to go on living together
- their partner has behaved in a way that it would be unreasonable to expect the spouse to continue living together
- their partner has deserted them for a period of two or more years
- they and their partner have been living separately for two years and both agree to divorce
- they and their partner have been living separately for five years or more whether or not the partner agrees to the divorce

Leaving home with the baby and a bag of belongings and going to this women's refuge may be a last desperate act after months or even years of violence in a marriage.

In the United States by 1983 every state except one made divorce available on a "no fault" basis. Laws vary from state to state but basically share the same principle of allowing couples to separate because of irreconcilable differences rather than requiring one to blame the other for some misdeed. In many states the laws have been simplified so that couples can arrange their own divorce without involving attorneys. This means that the financial cost of divorce has been reduced considerably.

Nevertheless most couples do turn to lawyers when they run into difficulties or cannot agree and in Britain it is necessary to have a solicitor in almost all situations. Those who cannot afford one can apply for legal aid. Depending on the attitude of the couple and the approach of the solicitor – some are conciliatory, others approach divorce as a battle – the couple may be able to negotiate a settlement out of court. This will cover the division of property, finances and, of course, the care of children. Settling matters out of court is not only the most civilised and least expensive way, it is also more likely to give both partners an outcome with which they are satisified. If the couple reach an agreement that is acceptable to the court then the issuing of the divorce is something of a formality. If they cannot agree then the case goes before a judge. Contesting a divorce case through the courts can be a very long and very expensive business which may lead to no one getting what they want.

> **"By the time we had each paid an attorney, there wasn't much money left."**

Where there are children involved the judge must be satisfied that arrangements for their care are adequate. If parents have agreed on custody (legal responsibility), care and control (day-to day care and where the children live) and access arrangements (visiting arrangements for the other parent), then this interview is just a formality. If parents cannot agree, the judge can send parents to conciliation.

Finding common ground

Conciliation, or mediation as it is sometimes called, is carried out usually either by court welfare officers or an outside agency and aims to help parents find common ground and arrive at workable arrangements for the children. If parents still cannot agree, the judge will order a welfare report to be made by the court welfare officer who will talk to the adults involved with the children and sometimes to the children themselves. On the basis of this the judge will make decisions about the children. In the United States about half the states have some kind of mediation service and

As a mother in dispute over the custody of her child in the film *Kramer versus Kramer*, Meryl Streep has to face the ordeal of arguing her case in court.

where these do not exist, the judge can ask for recommendations from a custody evaluator. California is the first state to require family mediation for all disputes over custody and visitation (access). Other states are likely to adopt a similar approach. Where disputes are resolved through conciliation or mediation, parents are likely to be on far better terms than if they have "fought" their case through the courts and arrangements for the children stand a better chance of working on a day-to-day basis. Couples can go voluntarily to conciliation as soon as they decide they want a divorce.

Conciliators usually work in pairs with a couple seeing them for anything from one to six sessions. Different agencies have different approaches, but they all aim to help the couple put aside their relationship as husband and wife and focus on their roles as parents. In order to do this, it may be necessary to allow them to air their differences and acknowledge the hurt and anger that they feel. But this is not the main purpose.

Older children are sometimes included in the sessions. Even when they are not, the couple will spend time looking at ways of helping their children deal with their fears and anxieties and understand the divorce.

Ideally, at the end of conciliation a couple will reach agreement about custody, access and possibly maintenance. Such an agreement is more likely to work than a solution inspired by the court. Children benefit from conciliation if it improves the relationship between their separating parents.

The courts' view

The courts have a great deal of discretion within the law as it stands and many people would like to see more imaginative arrangements worked out for custody and access. The courts tend to have a very conservative approach. This is reinforced by lawyers who advise parents to agree on arrangements that will be acceptable to the court. A psychologist or social worker might offer a very different view on what might be best for the children.

> **"However well you behave to start with, the law turns it into a battle. The way they call it 'Johnson versus Johnson', you know it's expected to be a fight."**

Custody

The courts tend to award custody and care and control (physical custody in the United States) to the mother on the basis that she is the most appropriate person to care for small children. But an increasing number of fathers are getting custody. Sometimes care and control is given to the mother and custody to both parents. More rarely, care and control may go to one parent and custody to the other.

Awarding custody to just one parent reinforces the win/lose nature of divorce. Children frequently lose contact with a non-custodial father. Research in California has shown that joint custody, even when it is imposed against the wishes of the parents, is less likely to lead to future disputes that have to be settled by the court.

The courts have certain fixed ideas on what are acceptable arrangements for children; brothers and sisters should not be split up; arrangements such as spending a month with one parent and a month with another are not regarded as satisfactory and until recently a homosexual father might be denied access to his children. None of these principles is backed by any research.

Access
Access arrangements (called visitation in the United States) ultimately depend on the goodwill and co-operation of parents but the courts could do more to stress its importance. They pay little attention to defining access, making orders in fewer than 50 per cent of cases and then often agreeing to the vague "reasonable" access.

Other cultures
Arrangements for ending marriage differ greatly from one country and one culture to another. In Sweden either partner can apply for divorce without having to give reasons. If both partners agree to the divorce and there are no children it will be granted immediately. Where one partner opposes the divorce or there are children involved, a six month period of reconsideration is required.

In Egypt, a muslim country, a husband can divorce his wife simply by going before a mazun - marriage registrar - and in the presence of witnesses declare that the marriage is ended. The couple can also go together but if a wife wants to end her marriage she has to go through a lengthy court procedure and demonstrate a breach of the marriage contract such as her husband's failure to provide for her financially. If he can demonstrate that he is providing for her then neither physical abuse nor a husband's adultery are seen as grounds for divorce.

Under Jewish law, divorce has been available ever since the 11th century. The divorce or "Get" is granted by rabbis and has to be handwritten in a special ceremony. The man then hands the Get to his wife. He must give it willingly and she must accept it willingly. Either party may refuse. Without a Get many Jewish Synagogues will not marry a couple if one or both have been divorced only by civil courts.

In Catholic countries although couples may be able to obtain a civil divorce, the church does not recognise divorce and re-marriage.

If this Muslim family were to divorce, it would be expected that the children would live with their mother while they were young but that the boys would go to live with their father once they were older.

CHAPTER 5

PAYING THE PRICE

"I couldn't
believe how petty
I was becoming.
We argued and
haggled over
every last one of
our possessions:
records, books,
plants, knives and
forks. I began to
hate myself and in
the end I said
'take what you
want. I don't
care'."

Divorce costs society a great deal financially. Some £100 million is spent every year on legal aid; many one parent families rely on state benefits; many children in care are from one parent families and it has been calculated that illness and distress following divorce lose industry more days off work than industrial disputes. And the cost to individuals is great both financially and emotionally.

Adults – the emotional costs

No one can walk away from a life shared over many years as though it had never happened. No matter how bad a relationship has become it takes time to separate from it. Often it is only one partner who wants the divorce. For them there is a great deal of stress in making the decision. Many months may be spent agonising over what to do. They may feel guilty, blame themselves and although separation is a relief they may be surprised that they still have strong feelings of loss or sadness.

> "I felt terribly guilty. Even though he had behaved so badly, I somehow thought it must be my fault. And when I thought of him alone in a bedsitter . . . but we couldn't stay together."

For the partner who is being divorced, the end of their marriage may come out of the blue. Their feelings of shock and grief are like those felt when a partner dies.

Even where both partners agree to divorce in a "civilized" arrangement there is still a sense of guilt and failure.

The legal process encourages bad feelings. One partner has to accuse the other of something in order to obtain a divorce. People are very dependent on their solicitors for guidance in what is likely to be a totally unfamiliar situation and ask advice on what to do for the best. Solicitors however can only advise in terms of what is possible in terms of the law. They see their role as protecting their client's interests and this inevitably sets up conflicts between partners. Many solicitors will try to minimise conflict and work in a conciliatory way, others do little to minimise the tensions between the couple.

Even a couple who thought they were reaching a civilised agreement can find themselves in bitter conflict pouring all kinds of old resentments and anger about the marriage into a battle over dividing up the home, the money and worst of all, the children.

> "I couldn't believe how petty I was becoming. We argued and haggled over every last one of our possessions: records, books, plants, knives and forks. I began to hate myself and in the end I said 'take what you want, I don't care'."

Some people suffer from depression following a divorce, some take to drink, others embark on one relationship after another but eventually most adults adjust to their divorced state and get on with their lives. Of those divorcing under 30, nearly 80 per cent have re-married within five years.

The financial cost

Society no longer expects a man to support his divorced wife indefinitely. The idea of the "clean break" – making a once and for all settlement compensating a wife for any earnings, promotion, or pension rights lost through having given up work to run a home - has gained acceptance in many countries including Britain and the United States. This may sound fine in principle but once there are children involved things become more difficult. If the children live with their mother, and they do in 80 per cent of cases, how are their interests to be considered separately from hers?

The courts agree that the children must come first. But they have been criticised for failing to establish satisfactory principles for dealing with maintenance and not taking sufficient account of women's reduced earning ability when they have the care of children. In the United States, judges appear to assume that parents have equal financial responsibility for children ignoring women's reduced earning power and the cost of childcare. A study in Colorado showed that two-thirds of fathers were ordered to pay less per month to support their children than they paid in installments on their car.

When a settlement is reached there is often not enough money to go around and both men and women may feel aggrieved.

> "Once we sell the house, his half of the money will go to setting up with *her*. I resent that. The children and I didn't want the divorce, why should we suffer?"

CASE STUDY

David's wife Mary is divorcing him for unreasonable behaviour. He does not want a divorce. His children will probably live with Mary. She will either continue to live in their house or (more likely) it will be sold to finance two smaller homes. He will have the smaller one.

David feels that he is losing everything and on top of it all he will have to pay up to a third of his wages to support her and the children. How can he ever afford to re-marry? He feels it is not fair.

Mary is also worried about money. She spent six years at home looking after the children, now she has a poorly paid part-time job. David agrees she is the best person to look after the children so she will not be able to think of full-time work for a while. She has seen the figures about one parent families: 80 per cent live below the poverty line. She knows 80 per cent of ex-husbands are either behind with or not paying maintenance. She has filed for divorce but it was his violence that drove her to it. She feels it is not fair.

CHAPTER 6

THE COST TO CHILDREN

"We used to see
my Dad quite a bit
but not now. Gary
thinks he doesn't
like us anymore
but I think it's
because Mum
doesn't like his
girlfriend."

In Britain it is likely that about 20 per cent of children born in the 1970s will experience their parents' divorce. Today about 1.5 million children live in a one parent family. In the United States about 14 million children live in one parent families.

Although for adults divorce, however painful, is accepted as the best solution to a bad marriage, children rarely see it as a good thing. Nor does society.

All families are different, children are different. How they respond to divorce will vary with their age, the kind of person they are, the sorts of relationships they have with their parents before and, more importantly, after the divorce.

Explaining

For many children, the news that their parents are divorcing comes as a complete surprise. Many parents fail to explain to their children what is happening either because they are too upset themselves or because they imagine the children must know or because they feel the children will be upset and the least said the better. But however stormy their home life children, especially younger ones, accept it as normal.

When children are not told what is happening, or more importantly what will happen in the future, they may imagine the worst. Small children often feel they are to blame for Mum or Dad leaving, and are frightened that the other parent will also go. They become clingy, have nightmares, refuse to go to school and need endless reassurance. They may even become ill to create a

"I couldn't believe it when my Gran told me Mum and Dad were getting divorced They shouted at each other a lot but they had always done that. I didn't see why it meant we had to live somewhere different from my Dad."

family crisis which will bring the parents together again, even if it is only for a while.

Even when children welcome an end to arguments or violence they almost always have a fantasy that their parents will get back together and this can last even when one or both parents have a new partner. Older children tend to respond to divorce with anger, sadness and often depression. The anger may be expressed towards brothers and sisters rather than parents, though teenage children may be very angry and critical of the parent whom they feel has behaved badly. Teenage children often cope with the situation at home by throwing themselves into their own social life and school activities preferring not to be at home with depressed and preoccupied parents.

Being involved in activities with friends can help older children and distract from problems at home.

Keeping in touch

After the first anger and distress, how well children are able to adjust to their new situation will depend on a variety of things, the most important is their relationship with both parents. If both parents manage to reassure them that although the marriage has ended their parental relationship has not changed; if the children continue to see the parent they are not living with and if both parents can co-operate over decisions that affect them, then most children will in a matter of months or perhaps a year adjust to the new situation. Children who have a good relationship with both parents adapt more easily.

> **"We used to see my Dad quite a bit but not now. Gary thinks he doesn't like us anymore but I think it's because Mum doesn't like his girlfriend."**

Sadly this ideal situation is not always the case. Some parents cannot separate their relationship as partners from their roles as parents. Children are used as bargaining tools in a fight over custody. A parent may be so angry with their partner that they cannot bear to allow the children to see him or her or they may not be able to cope with their ex-spouse's new partner. This can also mean the end of contact with other relations such as grandparents who may be important to the children. Partners sometimes have fears of losing custody and having the children lured away by the other parent. Up to a half of children see their non-custodial parent infrequently or not at all.

A real relationship

Access is successful when it is regular even if not very frequent. A visit needs to be long enough for the visiting parent to build up a real relationship. Staying with a parent overnight once a month and telephoning in between may be better than a brief trip to the park every Saturday afternoon.

Living as part of a one-parent family for most children means that there is little cash spare for presents, for clothes and items such as school trips. Some children are proud of the way their parent copes but lack of money can certainly exclude some children from the activities their friends enjoy.

If a divorced father sees his children regularly and is involved in their day-to-day care he can remain an important part of their lives.

Talking it through

A very important source of support for children coping with divorce is someone to whom they can talk. It is unfortunate that at the time when children need most parenting, parents are in no state to be able to offer it. Children are usually well aware of this and will often protect their parents from their feelings, knowing that they will only be another burden.

> "My Mum used to sit downstairs and cry after we'd gone to bed – I felt I wanted to comfort her but I knew I'd cry too, I missed my Dad. There wasn't anything either of us could do".

Because children tend to hide their feelings it is easy for parents to believe, usually wrongly, that they are not upset.

Grandparents can be a major source of comfort for many children. Others find help from aunts, uncles, schoolteachers, neighbours and, among older children, friends. Children who have been able to talk about their feelings find it easier to come to terms with their situation.

There is no "right" answer for children. Some do undoubtedly suffer long term problems following a divorce, others adjust well. They would all prefer to have stayed as a family.

> "The lady from the court came and talked to us and asked who we would rather live with. Me and my sister couldn't answer, we just wanted us all to stay together as a family."

The little boy in the film *Kramer versus Kramer* seen here with his father (played by Dustin Hoffman) is, like many children, torn between the conflicting loyalties to both his parents. If he runs to his mother, does it mean he is rejecting his father?

CHAPTER 7

THE FUTURE

"The lady from the court came and talked to us and asked who we would rather live with. Me and my sister couldn't answer, we just wanted us all to stay together as a family."

Despite the high divorce rate in Britain and the United States there is no sign that marriage is on the decline. Around 95 per cent of the population will be married at some stage of their life. Although there is a great increase in the number of couples who are co-habiting – living together without getting married – it is only a small minority who see it as an alternative to marriage. Even in a country such as Sweden where one-third of babies are born outside of marriage most couples do eventually marry. In other developed countries living together is generally a stage before marriage to the same or a different partner.

These young unemployed men in Florida want the same things from life as everyone else. But if their plans include marriage they will start with a handicap. Unemployment is a significant factor in divorce.

Fewer marriages might end in divorce if couples had more realistic expectations of marriages and family life. Schools could offer not just sex education programmes but also social studies that included a look at marriage, its difficulties as well as pleasures, at child-rearing and the needs of children.

> **"I was unemployed when we got married so we had to live with her parents. We didn't know how difficult it would be. We might have been alright with a place of our own."**

When couples have problems they could be encouraged by, for instance, family doctors to seek help much sooner. It is often to their family doctor that one partner will first talk. But this would mean far more help would have to be available which in turn means investing money in appropriate agencies. At present there is a waiting list of six months for marriage guidance in many parts of Britain. In six months a marriage may have fallen apart.

It seems likely, however, because of expectations of modern marriages combined with social pressures, that a large number of marriages will end in divorce. Can the process of divorce be made less painful and destructive, especially for children? Adults, after all, choose to divorce. Children have the situation thrust upon them.

Improvements
Within the existing framework of the law, things could be improved by a greater use of joint

custody, more flexibility in living arrangements for children, a more conciliatory approach by all solicitors and a more extensive and earlier use of conciliation.

> "I really enjoy holidays with my dad, we went fishing last summer. I'd like to live with him but my brother wants to stay with my mum. So my mum says I have to stay too."

The living standard of one-parent families would be improved if all maintenance orders were paid. Perhaps the State should take over the collection of maintenance deducting it directly from wages. This is the system in Hungary.

Family Courts

At present divorce and issues related to finance and children may be dealt with in a magistrates court, a county court or the Family Division of the High Court. These courts operate a complicated and confusing system of different overlapping laws drawn up at different times. One way of reforming the system would be to set up family courts which would deal with any matter relating to family life and would operate a rationalised system of law. Rationalising the existing law is in itself a daunting task and first there has to be an agreement on the fundamental principles on which the law should be based.

A number of countries such as Germany operate Family Courts. Their emphasis is on conciliation. They focus on helping parents reach agreements together over all aspects of divorce with facilities

for counselling and special reports on children from appropriate professionals. If it becomes necessary to have a formal court hearing, the children's interests are represented by an independent lawyer. Family Courts would seem to be the only legal and appropriate way to deal with divorce and the sooner they are established, the better for all the parents and children involved in divorce each year. They may help to reduce the difficulties of starting a new life after divorce.

At least one of these children will have parents who divorce. Can we change the divorce process so that children get a better deal?

SOURCES OF HELP

If you are experiencing or have experienced your parents' divorce, talking about how you feel can help. Friends, relatives, a teacher or perhaps your doctor may give you the support you need.

If you feel you need to talk to someone quite independent, ask at your local Citizen's Advice Bureau to see if there is a young people's counselling service near you. You can talk things through with someone there in complete confidence.

If you feel really desperate, or don't want to talk to anyone face to face, you can telephone ChildLine 0800-1111 or The Samaritans – their telephone number is in your local directory or ask the operator.

Advice and information on the law as it affects children can be obtained from:

The Children's Legal Centre,
20 Compton Terrace,
London N1 2UN
Telephone 01-359 6251

The centre publishes a handbook which although it is intended for adults advising young people, provides a clear guide to the complexities of the law on custody, access and maintenance.

There are a number of organisations which offer support to divorcing adults but parents do not always know about them:

National Family Conciliation Council,
34 Milton Road,
Swindon,
Wiltshire SN1 5JA
Telephone 0793 618486

They can supply details of conciliation services operating in the area where you live.

Stepfamily, the National Stepfamily Association links a network of self-help groups for parents with stepchildren. They are considering setting up a telephone counselling service for stepchildren.

Stepfamily,
162 Tenison Road,
Cambridge CB1 2DP
Telephone 0223 460312

Parents coping alone can get support from:

Gingerbread,
The Association for One Parent Families,
35, Wellington Street,
London WC2
Telephone 01-240 0953

For local groups see your telephone directory.

WHAT THE WORDS MEAN

access the British term for visitation, arrangements for the parent who does not have day-to-day care of the children to contact and visit them

adultery a sexual relationship outside marriage

alimony payment by one spouse to support the other, usually by the husband to the wife

annullment the cancelling of a marriage by either the church or state on the grounds that it was not valid

bigamy marrying again while still married

co-habitation living together as man and wife without marrying

conciliation helping a divorcing or separating couple to agree arrangements for caring for and supporting the children

custody the legal responsibility and right to make important decisions about the children's education, medical treatment, religion. Joint custody means that both parents continue to share the right. Sole custody gives the right to just one parent

desertion one spouse leaves home making no arrangements to continue to contribute financially or practically to the family

Get a Jewish divorce

illegitimate a child born to parents who are not married

legal aid payment by the state of legal fees

legal separation agreement between parents to live apart but not divorce

legitimate a child born to married parents and entitled to inherit their property

maintainance payment by a divorced partner to support their ex-spouse and children. Usually by a husband to a wife but it can be the other way round

mediation see conciliation

spouse a marriage partner, husband or wife

step-parent someone married to the biological parent of a child

visitation the American term for access

INDEX

Photographic Credits:

All the photographs are taken with models and obtained from the following agencies: Cover: Vanessa Bailey; pages 4, 6, 14, 17, 25, 29, 33, 35, 46, 51, 53 and 56: Rex Features; pages 9, 26, 36, 45, 49, 54 and 59: Richard and Sally Greenhill; page 11: Arkell/Network; page 12: Format; page 19: Lewis/Network; page 23: Sturrock/Network; page 30: Stern Magazine; page 40: Sparham/Network.